Life Lessons

Jennifer Moore-Mallinos
Illustrated by Gustavo Mazali

Money
doesn't grow on
trees!

BARRON'S

I couldn't believe my eyes! There I was walking through my neighborhood and on every tree, on every bush, in every park, in every yard, there were dollar bills hanging from every branch. Everywhere!!! It was the most wonderful sight I had ever seen. It was amazing!

2-3

Just to make sure my eyes weren't playing tricks on me, I ran over to all the bushes and trees to have a better look. And guess what? Not only was the money real, but the small bushes grew one dollar bills, the medium-sized trees grew five dollar bills, and the really big trees grew twenty dollar bills. Wow!!!

I was so excited! I ran into my house.

"Mom!," I yelled, "come quickly!"

Mom came running into the kitchen. "What's wrong?," she asked.

I jumped onto the counter and pointed out the window. "I can't believe all the money trees," I said.

Mom gave me a weird look. "Are you feeling alright?,"
she said as she felt my forehead, checking for a fever.
  "Those trees have always been there," she said.
  "What else would money trees grow?," Mom laughed.
"Sometimes you are so silly!"

I felt really mixed up because I couldn't remember trees ever growing money, but then I decided it didn't matter. For some crazy reason, money actually grew on trees. That was a dream come true.

"Mom, can I pick some money and buy that new video game I really want?" I asked.

"Of course," Mom said. "Whenever you want something new, like a new bike, a new scooter, or a new soccer ball, just pick what you need. You can have anything you want."

So that's exactly what I did. Before I knew it, our house gradually filled up with stuff. It looked like it was just about to burst! I bought every style of bike in every color, every kind of ball in every size, every video game, and even every kind of fishing rod. There was nothing else for me to want — I had it all!

At first, it was fun having everything I wanted, but then it just got way too hard. Not only did it take me a whole day to find all my bikes, but it also took me another whole day to ride them all and another whole day to put them all away again.

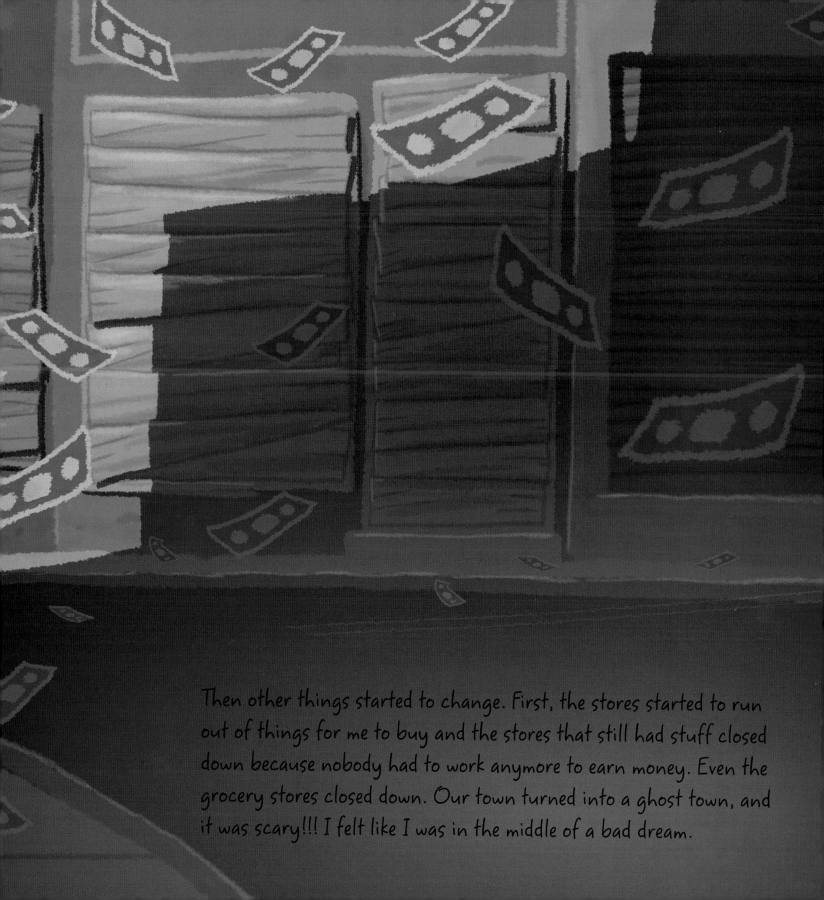

Then other things started to change. First, the stores started to run out of things for me to buy and the stores that still had stuff closed down because nobody had to work anymore to earn money. Even the grocery stores closed down. Our town turned into a ghost town, and it was scary!!! I felt like I was in the middle of a bad dream.

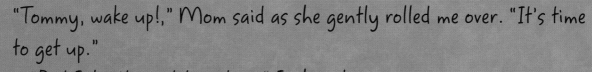

"Tommy, wake up!," Mom said as she gently rolled me over. "It's time to get up."

"But I don't want to get up," I whined.

"I thought you were trying to save up your money to buy that new basketball hoop you wanted," Mom said. "And before you can save any money, you first have to earn it."

Mom rubbed the top of my head, "Come on, we have to get to work. And money doesn't grow on trees you know."

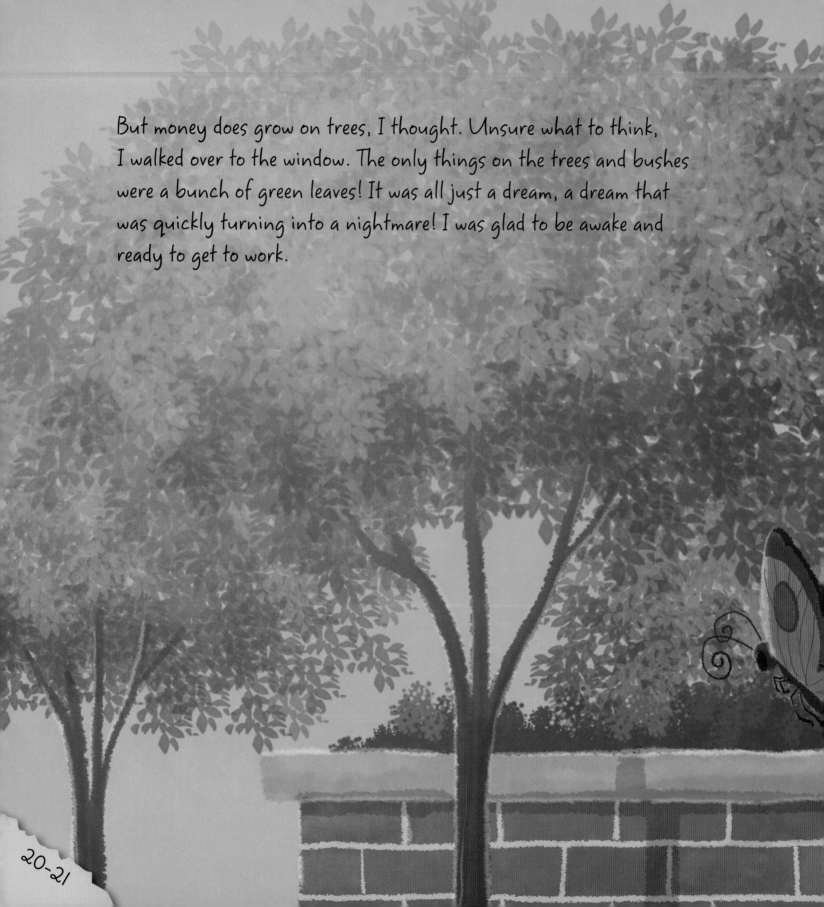

But money does grow on trees, I thought. Unsure what to think,
I walked over to the window. The only things on the trees and bushes
were a bunch of green leaves! It was all just a dream, a dream that
was quickly turning into a nightmare! I was glad to be awake and
ready to get to work.

From that day on, I went with Mom every Saturday to help at the market. I helped load and unload the truck, set up the table with all the fruits and vegetables, and also helped the shoppers by putting the things they bought into bags.

As I helped Mom set up our fruit and vegetable stand, I couldn't stop thinking about my dream. At first, it seemed so great being able to buy whatever I wanted without having to earn or save my money; but, when our town started to change, it scared me. Maybe it's not so bad, having to work hard to save up for the special things we want.

Then, at the end of the day, Mom and I sat down to count our money. Mom got most of it and I got the rest. Then we went to the bank so that I could put my money in a safe place. And guess what? I loved watching the money grow and grow in the bank. It helped me to continue working hard.

After a few weeks of hard work and saving my money, I had enough to buy that basketball hoop. Mom and I went to the sporting goods store to pick one out. I bought the hoop that I liked, and we took it home and set it up. I've since been having lots of fun shooting hoops with my friends.

Not only did it make me feel proud to be able to earn some money, but I also learned that money does not grow on trees! It takes hard work to make money and even harder work to save it.

Parents Guide

It's fun to imagine a world where the idea of working hard and saving money is not necessary. Having what you want when you want it, with no worries about how you are going to pay for it, sounds like an ideal situation at first.

But, unfortunately for almost all of us, this world does not exist. In fact, we do have to work hard and save our money for the things we need, let alone the things we want.

The idea of financial responsibility is unfamiliar to many of our children in today's society. Actually, many of our children have become used to a world where little effort is made in order to get the things they want. Therefore, the idea of working hard and saving money may be difficult for some to accept, but it is never too soon or too late to start teaching our children about the value of money and hard work.

Having what we want
when we want

The purpose of this book is thus to point out that working hard to save for the things we want is not a bad thing after all. It is okay to want things. In fact, this desire can be a positive force in creating a good work ethic and helping us to be careful with our money.

"Money Doesn't Grow on Trees!" is a great tool for starting dialogue and creating respect for money. Given ongoing economic problems, teaching our children the value of hard work, how to save and budget their money, and a sense of respect for the things we have is not only a valuable life lesson, but also a necessary one.

We get the result after working hard.

This book is a great tool for creating respect for money among children.

Money doesn't grow on trees!

Money doesn't grow on trees

First edition for the United States, its territories and dependencies, and Canada published in 2013 by Barron's Educational Series, Inc.

© Copyright 2012 by Gemser Publications, S.L.
El Castell, 38, 08329 Teià, Barcelona, Spain

Text: Jennifer Moore-Mallinos
Illustration: Gustavo Mazali
Design and layout: Estudi Guasch, S.L.

All inquiries should be addressed to:
Barron's Educational Series, Inc.
250 Wireless Boulevard
Hauppauge, NY 11788
www.barronseduc.com

ISBN: 978-1-4380-0349-8

Library of Congress Control Number: 2013931783

Date of Manufacture: July 2013
Place of Manufacture: L. REX PRINTING COMPANY LIMITED,
Dongguan City, Guangdong, China

Product conforms to all applicable
CPSC and CPSIA 2008 standards.
No lead or phthalate hazard.

Printed in China
9 8 7 6 5 4 3 2 1